PERCY JACKSON

THE ULTIMATE GUIDE

PUFFIN BOOKS

Published by the Penguin Group: London, New York, Australia, Canada, India, Ireland, New Zealand and South Africa
Penguin Books Ltd, Registered Offices:
80 Strand, London WC2R 0RL, England
puffinbooks.com

Based on the Percy Jackson series by Rick Riordan

First published by Hyperion Books, an imprint of Disney Book Group 2009
Published in Great Britain in Puffin Books 2010
10 9 8 7 6 5 4 3 2 1

Percy Jackson: The Ultimate Guide is created and manufactured by
Brushfire Books, London, England
Written by Mary-Jane Knight
Designed by Philip Chidlow for Brushfire Books
Additional illustration by Artful Doodlers, Philip Chidlow and Kevin Hays
All rights reserved
The moral right of the author and illustrators has been asserted
Brushfire Books are grateful for permission to reproduce copyright material. Whilst every effort has been made to
trace copyright holders Brushfire Books would be pleased to hear from any not acknowledged

British Library Cataloguing in Publication Data
A CIP catalogue record for this book is available from the British Library

Made and printed in China
ISBN: 978–0–141–33157–7

Percy Jackson

The Ultimate Guide

PUFFIN

RO PAE PA=

Talaurius
campus

CRO

NIVM

MARE.

NESTAEI.

ENCHELEAE

Cadmi Harmoniæq̃
monumentum

Oricum

LATIVM.

TVRRHE-
NIA.

Caieta

AVSO-
NIA.

RRHENVM AEQVOR

TRINACRIA.

IONIVM MARE.

DOLOPES.

THESSA-
LIA.

Locri.

ACHAIA.

PELOPIS
REGIO.

LIBYSTICVM MARE.

THR

4

CONTENTS

SECTION ONE

PERCY JACKSON

THE ULTIMATE GUIDE

PERCY JACKSON is far from average, even if his grades often are (well, technically, they're more like "below average"). His differences are not immediately obvious, but they become increasingly problematic once he reaches the age of twelve. Strange things begin to happen to him. He is attacked by monsters and befriended by a satyr. And that's just the beginning. Once he goes to Camp Half-Blood, a whole new world opens for him...

"Being a half-blood is dangerous. It's scary. Most of the time it gets you killed in painful, nasty ways... if you recognize yourself in these pages – if you feel something stirring inside... you might be one of us. And once you know that, it's only a matter of time before they sense it too, and they'll come for you. Don't say I didn't warn you."

—Percy Jackson

Name:	**Percy Jackson**
Birthday:	**August 18th**
Place of birth:	**New York**
Mother:	**Sally Jackson**
Father:	**Poseidon**
Favorite food:	**Anything blue and sweet**
Favorite drink:	**Coke and nectar**
Favorite place:	**Summer cabin at Montauk, Long Island**
Favorite form of transport:	**Pegasus (Blackjack)**
Best at:	**Sword-fighting**
Worst at:	**Spelling**
Friends:	**Grover Underwood, Annabeth, Tyson, Mrs. O'Leary**
Enemies:	**Kronos, Gabe Ugliano, Mrs. Dodds**

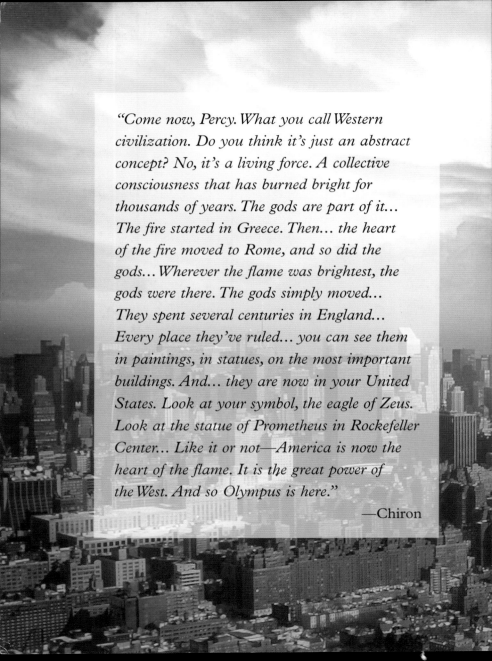

"*Come now, Percy. What you call Western civilization. Do you think it's just an abstract concept? No, it's a living force. A collective consciousness that has burned bright for thousands of years. The gods are part of it... The fire started in Greece. Then... the heart of the fire moved to Rome, and so did the gods... Wherever the flame was brightest, the gods were there. The gods simply moved... They spent several centuries in England... Every place they've ruled... you can see them in paintings, in statues, on the most important buildings. And... they are now in your United States. Look at your symbol, the eagle of Zeus. Look at the statue of Prometheus in Rockefeller Center... Like it or not—America is now the heart of the flame. It is the great power of the West. And so Olympus is here.*"

—Chiron

MT. OLYMPUS

"I'm twelve years old. Until a few months ago, I was a boarding student at Yancy Academy, a private school for troubled kids in upstate New York. Am I a troubled kid? Yeah. You could say that."

PARENTS, OR LACK OF THEM

SALLY JACKSON

Percy's mother. Has long brown hair streaked with gray, eyes the color of the sea, and a smile as warm as a quilt. Sally was orphaned at an early age...

MYSTERY PLANE CRASH ORPHANS CHILD

Reports were coming in last night that at least one child has been orphaned as a result of the devastating plane crash in New York State yesterday. Sally Jackson, age five, is the only daughter of Jim and Laura Jackson. Both are known passengers on the plane which came down in a field 150 miles south of Lake Ontario at 3AM yesterday morning. No survivors have been found and the cause of the crash is as yet unknown.

Neighbors of the Jacksons have paid tribute to "the lovely family who always had time for everyone" and were respected members of the community. Sally is reported to be staying with an uncle until her future can be decided.

My dear Sally

It breaks my heart to write you this note, but I have no one else to turn to. I know how well you've been doing at high school and how hard you've worked to get to college. But now I know there is nothing more the doctors can do to help me and my health insurance has run out. You're my only hope... could you take a semester or two off to look after your poor old uncle till he finally departs this world?

Uncle Rich

Sally was never married to Percy's father, but she tells Percy that meeting his father was the best thing that ever happened to her. Percy's dad was a rich and important man and their relationship was secret. One day he set sail across the Atlantic and never returned... So Sally raised Percy on her own.

"My mom is the nicest lady in the world. She should've been married to a millionaire, not to some jerk like Gabe."

GABE UGLIANO

When Sally worked in a candy store in Grand Central Terminal, she married Gabe Ugliano, a fat, bald, beer-drinking cigar smoker, known to Percy as Smelly Gabe because he reeked like moldy garlic pizza wrapped in gym shorts. Gabe managed an Electronics Mega-Mart, usually from home while he played cards with his cronies. He bullied Percy, demanding money from him to feed his gambling habit.

BAD EVENTS IN PERCY'S EARLY LIFE

• A very young Percy Jackson was having a nap at nursery school when a snake slithered up to him. No one knew until his mom came to pick him up and found Percy playing with the dead snake which he had strangled.

• In third grade a man in a black trenchcoat stalked him on the playground. When teachers threatened to call the police he went away growling. No one believed Percy when he told them the man had only one eye in the middle of his forehead.

EXPELLED

Percy has had trouble with school for as long as he can remember. By age twelve he'd been to six schools in as many years because he kept getting kicked out. He'd been diagnosed with dyslexia and attention-deficit hyperactivity disorder (ADHD), but those weren't his only obstacles—inexplicable things happened to him at school and on field trips.

PERCY'S BLUNDERS

• In fourth grade his class went on a behind-the-scenes tour of the Marine World shark pool. Percy hit the wrong lever by the catwalk they were walking along, and the whole class took an unplanned swim with the sharks.

• In fifth grade he visited the Saratoga battlefield and had an accident involving a Revolutionary War cannon. He claimed he wasn't aiming for the school bus, but it took a direct hit anyway, and that meant yet another expulsion.

REPORT CARD

Student: *Percy Jackson*

General Comments:

ENGLISH   Grade F   Must try harder
Consistently fails to complete reading assignments.
When writing, has difficulty in expressing himself
clearly. Has only a notional grasp of spelling, and
the legibility of his handwriting leaves a great deal to
be desired.

MATH   Grade C   Pay attention in class!
Has mastered basic arithmetic, but lacks the interest
and concentration to progress in this subject.

HISTORY   Grade D   More effort
Often tries in class, but is hindered by his inability to
concentrate for more than a few minutes at a time.
He made a good attempt at describing some Civil War
events, but a little more historical analysis and a little
less battlefield gore would be appropriate.

SCIENCE   Grade B-   Must control himself!
Excels at practical experiments, but should refrain
from blowing up labs and igniting teacher's hair...

THE FIELD TRIP TO END ALL TRIPS

Percy's sixth-grade field trip was with his classmates at the Yancy Academy. They visited the Metropolitan Museum. It was here that the extraordinary events began which eventually led Percy to Camp Half-Blood.

YANCY CHARACTERS

Nancy Bobofit: freckled, redheaded, kleptomaniac. Percy's chief tormentor and the catalyst for the shocking events at the museum.

Grover: Percy's best friend; the only sixth-grader with acne and a wispy beard. Curly brown hair. Excused from PE because of a muscular disease in his legs.

Mr. Brunner: Percy's Latin teacher, middle-aged, in a motorized wheelchair. Thinning hair, scruffy beard. Wears a frayed tweed jacket and tells stories and jokes in class. Has a collection of Roman weapons.

Mrs. Dodds: mean math teacher, always wears a black leather jacket and dislikes Percy. At the museum she transforms into a shrivelled hag with yellow fangs and attacks Percy.

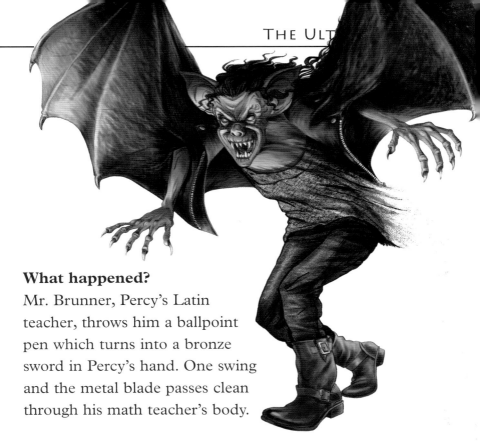

What happened?

Mr. Brunner, Percy's Latin teacher, throws him a ballpoint pen which turns into a bronze sword in Percy's hand. One swing and the metal blade passes clean through his math teacher's body.

"Mrs. Dodds was a sand castle in a power fan. She exploded into yellow powder, vaporized on the spot, leaving nothing but the smell of sulphur and a dying screech and a chill of evil in the air, as if those two glowing red eyes were still watching me."

19

THE FURIES

THE FURIES, OR THE ERINYES, ARE THREE CRUEL EARTH GODDESSES OF REVENGE AND RETRIBUTION. THEY ARE TERRIFYING-LOOKING CREATURES WITH HORRIBLE FEATURES. THEIR BREATH BURNS AND POISONOUS BLOOD DRIPS FROM THEIR EYES. THEIR HEADS ARE WREATHED IN SNAKES.

IN GREEK MYTHS THE ERINYES WERE SISTERS. THEIR NAMES WERE ALECTO (THE ANGRY ONE), MEGAERA (THE GRUDGING ONE) AND TISIPHONE (THE AVENGER). THEY PUNISHED CRIMES SUCH AS MURDER AND INJUSTICE, AND THEY WERE REPUTED TO CONTINUE PUNISHING A SINNER, EVEN AFTER HIS DEATH, UNTIL HE SHOWED REMORSE.

THE THREE FATES

THE FATES ARE THREE GREEK GODDESSES OF DESTINY AND FATE, ALSO KNOWN AS THE MOIRAE. THEY ARE TIMELESS OLD HAGS WHO WEAVE THE THREADS OF DESTINY THAT CONTROL EVERYONE'S LIFE. THEIR NAMES ARE CLOTHO, WHO SPINS THE THREAD OF LIFE, LACHESIS WHO ALLOTS THE LENGTH OF THE YARN, AND ATROPOS WHO SNIPS THE THREAD AND DECIDES WHEN LIFE WILL END.

ALL THE GOOD AND EVIL THAT BEFALLS EVERYONE IS WOVEN INTO THEIR DESTINY AND CANNOT BE ALTERED. THE FATES CONTROL THE DESTINIES OF ALL. EVEN THE GREATEST GODS ARE SUBJECT TO THEIR DECISIONS.

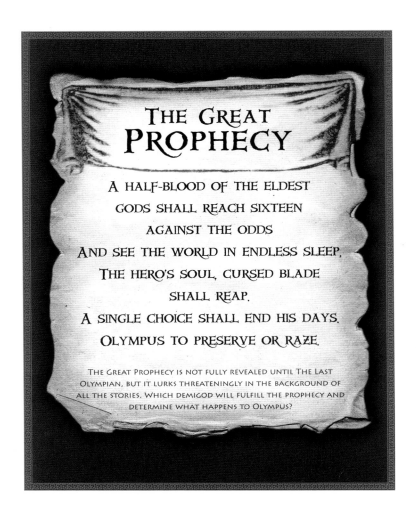

The Great
PROPHECY

A HALF-BLOOD OF THE ELDEST
GODS SHALL REACH SIXTEEN
AGAINST THE ODDS
AND SEE THE WORLD IN ENDLESS SLEEP,
THE HERO'S SOUL, CURSED BLADE
SHALL REAP.
A SINGLE CHOICE SHALL END HIS DAYS,
OLYMPUS TO PRESERVE OR RAZE.

THE GREAT PROPHECY IS NOT FULLY REVEALED UNTIL THE LAST
OLYMPIAN, BUT IT LURKS THREATENINGLY IN THE BACKGROUND OF
ALL THE STORIES. WHICH DEMIGOD WILL FULFILL THE PROPHECY AND
DETERMINE WHAT HAPPENS TO OLYMPUS?

SECTION TWO

LIFE AT CAMP

THE ULTIMATE GUIDE

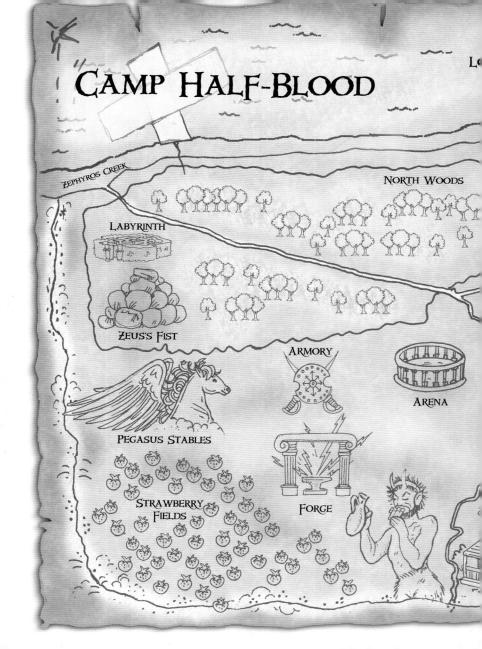

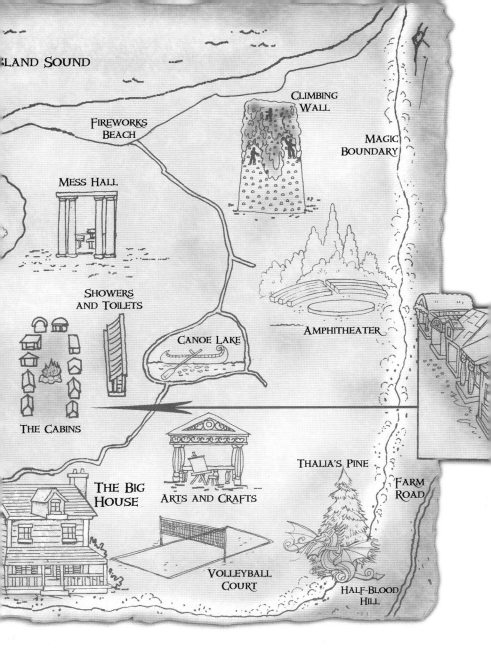

DREAMS

Dreams play an important part in the life of a demigod. Often they offer a glimpse of events happening elsewhere, or take the dreamer into the lives of their enemies or the friends they are searching for. The night before Percy enters Camp Half-Blood, he has this terrifying dream:

"It was storming on the beach, and two beautiful animals, a white horse and a golden eagle, were trying to kill each other at the edge of the surf. The eagle swooped down and slashed the horse's muzzle with its huge talons. The horse reared up and kicked at the eagle's wings. As they fought, the ground rumbled, and a monstrous voice chuckled ... goading the animals to fight harder. I ran toward them, knowing I had to stop them ... but I was running in slow motion. I knew I would be too late. I saw the eagle dive down, its beak aimed at the horse's wide eyes, and I screamed, No!"

PERCY'S FIRST MONSTER

Percy's mom and Grover jump into Smelly Gabe's Camaro and try to get Percy to Camp Half-Blood where he will be safe. But first, he has to confront his first real monster, a massive, angry bull-man.

"His neck was a mass of muscle and fur leading up to his enormous head, which had a snout as long as my arm, snotty nostrils with a gleaming brass ring, cruel black eyes, and horns – enormous black-and-white horns with points you just couldn't get from an electric sharpener..."

This is the first true test of Percy's mettle... How will he survive, and can he protect both Grover and his mother?

THESEUS AND THE MINOTAUR

THE MINOTAUR WAS A MONSTER WITH THE HEAD OF A BULL AND THE BODY OF A MAN. HE WAS THE SON OF THE WIFE OF KING MINOS OF CRETE, AND A BULL SENT TO MINOS BY POSEIDON.

MINOS ASKED DAEDALUS TO BUILD A PALACE WITH A HUGE MAZE OF ROOMS IN WHICH HE KEPT THE MONSTER IMPRISONED. EVERY YEAR HE FED IT WITH SEVEN YOUNG MEN AND SEVEN GIRLS SENT FROM ATHENS.

ONE YEAR THESEUS, THE SON OF AEGEUS, THE KING OF ATHENS, WENT TO CRETE WITH THE OTHER YOUNG MEN, HAVING VOWED THAT HE WOULD KILL THE MINOTAUR. KING MINOS'S DAUGHTER ARIADNE FELL IN LOVE WITH THESEUS AND GAVE HIM A BALL OF THREAD WHICH ALLOWED HIM TO ESCAPE FROM THE LABYRINTH ONCE HE HAD KILLED THE MONSTER.

"*He picked up Gabe's Camaro by the torn roof, the chassis creaking and groaning. He raised the car over his head and threw it down the road. It slammed into the wet asphalt and skidded in a shower of sparks for about half a mile before coming to a stop. The gas tank exploded. Not a scratch, I remembered Gabe saying. Oops.*"

CAMP HALF-BLOOD

Once Percy recovers from his dramatic arrival at camp, he begins to realize that this is definitely not a normal summer camp. Although he is pleased to find Grover there with him, he is shocked to discover that his best friend is a satyr. And this is just the beginning of a series of unsettling revelations.

When Percy is invited to join in a game of pinochle with his former Latin teacher, the truth about Camp Half-Blood and much more is revealed.

TEN SIGNS

THAT YOU MAY BE A

HALF-BLOOD

THE TEN SIGNS

Make a note of how many times you agree with the following statements.

1. You have suspicions that at least one of your teachers may not be human.

In itself, this proves nothing, as many teachers are some form of monster in disguise. Do watch out for teachers with an unnatural interest in torturing you, though.

2. You have been tested for, and diagnosed with, ADHD.

ADHD, or attention-deficit hyperactivity disorder, doesn't mean that you never pay attention. It could be that you have difficulty in filtering out the sights and sounds around you when your teacher drones on about something which doesn't interest you. So watching a dryad and a satyr chatting under the weeping willow outside the classroom window may grab your attention when your teacher would prefer you to be writing notes. This can result in shouting and punishments.

Your energy levels (or hyperactivity) may make it difficult for you to sit still through a whole class. You may also find that you have a tendency to do or say the first thing that comes into your mind. Young demigods frequently experience these symptoms, which show that they have superior fighting skills and reflexes, which can keep them alive when battling monsters.

3. You have been tested for, and diagnosed with, dyslexia.

Dyslexia causes problems with reading and writing. You are just as clever as other kids, but your brain finds it difficult to process written information. Reading can feel like torture and words seem to float off the page. In many cases, half-blood kids see things that ordinary kids just can't see. Their brains are hard-wired to interpret ancient Greek, which is why they have problems with decoding modern languages.

4. Odd events have occurred which you cannot explain.

These might be something not completely out of the ordinary, such as an adult behaving oddly, then denying later that they did anything unusual. Or it can cover truly dramatic events such as a demon attacking your school bus, or an unexplained explosion in the science lab. Any mysterious event of this sort could be a sign that you can see through the Mist, which is the veil that stops humans from seeing what really happens when monsters are around. The more often you have glimpses through the Mist, the more likely it is that you have Olympian blood in your veins.

5. You often experience déjà vu.

Half-bloods frequently have a sense that they have been through an experience before, even though they know it's the first time it has happened. This is because they experience time differently from ordinary humans. So you may feel that time slows down, for example, if you are in danger of being attacked by a monster, or when tackling pages of math problems at school.

Alternatively, time can seem to speed up, for example, when you are trying to evade a pack of hellhounds, or when you're playing capture the flag. All these experiences point to the presence of immortal blood in your veins, and they relate to your destiny as a demigod. If you were at camp on Half-Blood Hill, they would be a sign that you should consult the Oracle.

6. At times it seems unlikely that your father or your mother is really your parent.

Most human kids dream at some time or another that their parents may not be their real parents, but this may actually be true for half-bloods. A mortal parent will try to keep the truth from a half-blood for as long as possible because of the risks and unhappiness that can be part of life when you are the child of a god. Also, it could be that your parent is embarrassed to admit that she or he had a relationship with a god, although this behavior is not technically illegal (except in Mississippi).

7. *One or more of your friends doesn't seem quite normal.*
You may have detected the school satyr. Most schools have at least one, who may befriend you. Look out for hair big enough to cover small goat horns; an appetite for more or less anything; a bleating laugh; desperate attempts to keep their legs covered at all times. Some satyrs pass for humans more easily than others, but there is always one clue or another to their real identity.

8. *When you are alone, you have a strange sensation of being watched or followed, although no one is there.*
You may simply be a hyper-sensitive mortal. Or you could be under surveillance by monsters. They have been reported hiding in attics, basements, closets and school restrooms, as well as anywhere there is thick, concealing undergrowth.

9. Your dreams are different from those of your friends and you seem to be able to control what happens in them, or you experience a particularly vivid recurring dream.

Most half-bloods are sent signs and portents when they are asleep, unlike ordinary mortals. Demigods can also control their dreams, deciding mid-nightmare that they'd rather not suffer torture by monsters in an underground cell, preferring instead to dream about the pleasures of a pig-roasting luau in Elysium.

10. You suffer from irrational fears or phobias, for example, being afraid of heights, water, the dark, or spiders.

An irrational fear may be more rational than you think and can be connected to demigod status. Half-bloods may fear anything their Olympian parents hate. For example, the children of Hephaestus are afraid of high places and have nightmares about falling. This comes from the god's childhood, when he was thrown from Mount Olympus by Zeus. The children of Athena fear spiders, a direct result of the goddess's unpleasant run-in with Arachne, who Athena turned into a spider.

RESULTS

If you agreed with 8 or more statements, there is a strong possibility that you are a half-blood. Take great care and look for help on or before your twelfth birthday.

If you agreed with between 5 and 7 statements: you are a borderline risk. There may be some Olympian blood in your family, or you could be the child of a minor god or goddess. You will probably be able to live happily in the mortal world, unless your symptoms become more acute.

If you agreed with between 3 and 4 statements: you are unlikely to be a half-blood. Your imagination may be unusually active and you might be especially receptive to the world of monsters and half-bloods.

If you agreed with between 0 and 2 statements: you can rest assured that you are completely human and are unlikely ever to encounter monsters or Olympian gods except in books.

THE TRUTH ABOUT MR. BRUNNER

At Camp Half-Blood Percy discovers that
Mr. Brunner's real name is Chiron, and he's a skilled
pinochle player. But that's not all that Percy learns
about his former Latin teacher...

*"At first, I thought he was wearing very long, white
underwear, but as he kept rising out of the chair, taller than
any man, I realized that the velvet underwear... was the
front of an animal, muscle and sinew under coarse white
fur... A leg came out, long and knobbly-kneed, with a huge
polished hoof. Then another front leg, then hindquarters, and
then the box was empty, nothing but a metal shell with a
couple of fake human legs attached. I stared at the horse who
had just sprung from the wheelchair: a huge white stallion.
But where its neck should be was the upper body of my Latin
teacher, smoothly grafted to the horse's trunk.*

*'What a relief,' the centaur said. 'I'd been cooped up in
there so long, my fetlocks had fallen asleep.'"*

CENTAURS

CENTAURS HAD THE TORSO AND HEAD OF A MAN AND THE BODY OF A HORSE. THEY FOLLOWED DIONYSUS, THE GOD OF WINE.

THE CENTAURS LIVED ON MOUNT PELION IN THESSALY, NORTHERN GREECE. THEY HAD A REPUTATION FOR DRUNKENNESS AND BAD BEHAVIOR. THE EXCEPTION WAS THE MOST FAMOUS CENTAUR OF ALL, CHIRON, WHO WAS WISE, GENTLE, AND A RENOWNED TEACHER.

CHIRON WAS THE IMMORTAL SON OF THE TITAN KRONOS. HE TAUGHT ASCHLEPIUS, THE GOD OF HEALING, AS WELL AS THE GREEK HEROES ACHILLES, JASON, AND THESEUS.

PEGASI

A PEGASUS IS A WINGED HORSE (PLURAL *PEGASI*). THE NAME PEGASUS COMES FROM THE GREEK WORD FOR SPRING. LEGEND TELLS HOW THE FIRST PEGASUS SPRANG FROM THE NECK OF THE GORGON SLAIN BY THE DEMIGOD PERSEUS. HE WAS THE SON OF THE GORGON AND POSEIDON, AND WHEREVER HIS HOOF STRUCK THE GROUND, A SPRING FLOWED. THE PEGASUS FLEW TO OLYMPUS AND BROUGHT THUNDERBOLTS TO ZEUS.

PERCY'S MAIN STEED IS A PEGASUS CALLED BLACKJACK. HE IS A PURE BLACK STALLION WITH WINGS LIKE A GIANT RAVEN. BLACKJACK HELPS PERCY ON SEVERAL QUESTS, ALONG WITH HIS TWO FRIENDS, GUIDO AND PORKPIE.

.F-BLOOD

MEET THE CAMPERS

"Immortals are constrained by ancient rules. But a hero can go anywhere, challenge anyone, as long as he has the nerve."

ANNABETH CHASE

Daughter of Athena, goddess of wisdom, war, and useful arts. Blonde curly hair, gray eyes, athletic, deep tan. At Camp Half-Blood longer than any camper. Planner and strategist.

LUKE CASTELLAN

Son of Hermes, god of travelers. Was once the head of the Hermes cabin. Tall, muscular, short-cropped sandy hair. Thick white scar runs from beneath right eye to jaw. Skilled swordsman.

CLARISSE LA RUE

Daughter of Ares, god of war. Long brown hair, extremely strong. Aggressive and a fearsome fighter.

SILENA BEAUREGARD

Daughter of Aphrodite, goddess of love and beauty. Was head of the Aphrodite cabin. Slim, pretty, blue eyes, blonde hair.

ANNABETH ▶

CHARLES BECKENDORF

Son of Hephaestus, the god of fire and crafts. Was head of the Hephaestus cabin. Huge, well-built. Excellent armorsmith and ingenious mechanic.

CONNOR STOLL

Son of Hermes and brother of Travis. Tall, skinny, mop of curly brown hair, crooked smile, shorter than his brother. Nice guy, but big on practical jokes.

TRAVIS STOLL

Son of Hermes and older brother of Connor. Curly hair, crooked smile, a few inches taller than Connor. Similarly fond of jokes.

"...they had those elfish features all Hermes's kids had: upturned eyebrows, sarcastic smiles, and a gleam in their eyes whenever they looked at you – like they were about to drop a firecracker down your shirt."

CHRIS RODRIGUEZ

Son of Hermes. At one time abandoned camp to join the Titan army.

THALIA GRACE

Daughter of Zeus. Turned into a pine tree but later returned to human form. Short dark hair, electric blue eyes, freckles. Lithe, strong, always wears black clothes. Joined the Hunters of Artemis. *"If you've never seen Thalia run into battle, you've never been truly frightened."*

MICHAEL YEW

Son of Apollo, god of prophecy, music and healing. Was in charge of Apollo cabin. Short, with pointed nose and scrunched up features. Scowls a lot.

MALCOLM

Son of Athena. Annabeth's deputy in Athena cabin.

LEE FLETCHER

Son of Apollo.

KATIE GARDNER

Daughter of Demeter, goddess of agriculture.

JAKE MASON

Son of Hephaestus.

CASTOR AND POLLUX

Twin sons of Dionysus.

WILL SOLACE

Son of Apollo and a healer.

CAMP CHARACTERS

ARGUS
Head of security. Blue eyes cover his entire body.

ORACLE
Had the mummified body of a woman and spoke prophecies. She sat on a three-legged stool in the attic of the big house at Camp Half-Blood.
"A green mist poured from the mummy's mouth, coiling over the floor in thick tendrils, hissing like twenty thousand snakes... The mummy wasn't alive. She was some kind of gruesome receptacle for something else, the power that was now swirling around me in the green mist."

NAIADS
Water maidens who live in lakes and rivers. Percy encounters them at the bottom of the canoe lake at Camp Half-Blood.

Annabeth warns him that they are flirts who should not be encouraged.

"I noticed two teenage girls sitting cross-legged at the base of the pier, about twenty feet below. They wore blue jeans and shimmering green T-shirts, and their brown hair floated loose around their shoulders as minnows darted in and out. They smiled and waved as if I were a long lost friend."

DRYADS

Live in the forest. Dryads are the spirits of trees. Grover's girlfriend Juniper is a dryad who lives in a juniper tree.

"She was small... with wispy hair the color of amber and a pretty, elfish face. She wore a green chiton and laced sandals."

HESTIA (see also page 71)
Hestia is goddess of the hearth, and Percy first meets her in the form of a nine-year-old girl tending the fire at camp. She has brown hair and wears a brown dress and a headscarf. When campers sacrifice a portion of their meals to the gods, she receives a share as the tender of the flame.

SATYRS

Satyrs have the upper body of a man (but with horns in their hair) and the lower body of a goat. They can smell both monsters and half-bloods and talk to animals. There is a satyr in every school, with the job of finding half-bloods and escorting them to Camp Half-Blood.

GROVER UNDERWOOD

Became Percy's best friend at Yancy Academy, where he'd gone to find him and bring him to Camp Half-Blood. Accompanies Percy on quests. Grover and Percy have an empathy link which allows them to communicate when they're miles apart. Although the main role of a satyr is to bring half-bloods safely to Camp Half-Blood, Grover's life ambition was always to become the satyr who discovered the god Pan, lord of the wild. To do this he needed a Searcher's Licence from the Council of Cloven Elders.

GROVER'S SKILLS
PAN PIPES

Like all satyrs, Grover plays the pan pipes. The satyrs at Camp Half-Blood play their pan pipes in the strawberry fields to repel insect pests. Grover knows very few tunes when Percy first meets him, but gradually becomes more skilled, and eventually uses his pipes in several sticky situations.

ACORN TRACKING

Grover carries acorns which rearrange themselves in a pattern on the ground while he plays his pan pipes. He reads the pattern to decide what to do and where to go.

SATYR'S SANCTUARY

This is a goat blessing that Grover bestows on animals to grant them safe passage in the wild.

SATYR FACTS

All satyrs:
• Can smell monsters.
• Hate being underground.
• Dislike cyclopes (the feeling is mutual).
• Are not happy at sea.
• Favorite food: everything, including enchiladas, jellybeans, tin cans, and especially Louis XVI furniture.

"Grover opened his mouth, and the most horrible sound I'd ever heard came out. It was like a brass trumpet magnified a thousand times – the sound of fear."

DETECT A SATYR

Could there be a satyr in your life?
If you suspect there may be, ask yourself the
following questions:

• Does someone you know have odd eating
habits, sometimes nibbling on soda cans
rather than just drinking the contents?
• Does this person always wear long pants
or jeans?
• Do they walk as though every step hurts?
• Do they have an especially acute sense of smell?
• Do they smell like a wet wool sweater when they
get caught in the rain?

If you answered yes to three or more of these
questions, you may want to peek under the
suspect's covers while they sleep to check on
their feet.

CYCLOPES

Cyclopes are giant one-eyed monsters whose name means 'circle eye.' Legend says that they were so ugly that their father locked them away in the Underworld.

When Zeus beat Kronos in the War of the Titans (see page 62), the Cyclopes were freed and became the makers of Zeus's dreaded thunderbolts. They were skilled workers and also made Poseidon's trident and Hades's helm, as well as a silver bow and arrows for Artemis.

They lived underground, making weapons in the forges of the gods and were immune to fire. They had excellent hearing, could smell monsters, and speak in others' voices.

TYSON

Son of Poseidon, and half-brother to Percy, who takes on the Colchis bulls (see page 138) when they threaten Camp Half-Blood.

Tyson becomes a useful member of the quest to rediscover the Golden Fleece, during which they encounter Polyphemus. Poseidon calls Tyson to work in his undersea forges, where he proves himself to be a brilliant metal-worker, making Percy magical weapons and a wristwatch that turns into a war shield.

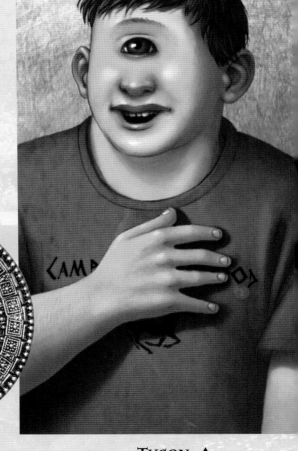

TYSON ▲

PERCY'S ACTIVITY SCHEDULE

	MON	TUES
08:00-09:00	Breakfast and cabin inspection	Breakfast and cabin inspection
09:00-10:30	Ancient Greek	Ancient Greek
10:30-11:00	Lunch preparation	Store checks
11:00-12:00	Archery	Javelin throwing
12:00-12:30	Greek mythology	Greek mythology
12:30-13:30	Lunch	Lunch
13:30-15:30	Weapon-making	Ride the rapids
15:30-17:00	Letters home	Cabin clean-up
17:00-18:00	Free time	Free time
18:00-19:00	Dinner	Dinner
19:00-21:00	Volleyball league	Unarmed combat
21:00-22:00	Campfire singalong	Campfire singalong

Morning cabin inspections: *Carried out by senior camp counselors in rotation*
Ancient Greek/Greek mythology: *Taught by Chiron and Annabeth*
Sword-fighting: *In the arena*

Weapon-making: *At the forge with Hephaestus cabin*
Archery: *With Chiron*
Wrestling: *With Clarisse*
Dog-handling: *With Mrs. O'Leary*

WED	THURS	FRI
Breakfast and cabin inspection	Breakfast and cabin inspection	Breakfast and cabin inspection
Ancient Greek	Ancient Greek	Ancient Greek
Cleaning stables	Picking strawberries	Polishing armor
Sword skills	Monster assault techniques	Pegasus riding
Greek mythology	Greek mythology	Greek mythology
Lunch	Lunch	Lunch
Tracking skills	Wrestling	Volleyball
Laundry	Wood-chopping	Firework-making
Free time	Free time	Free time
Dinner	Dinner	Dinner
Archery knockout	Trials of strength	Capture the flag
Campfire singalong	Campfire singalong	Campfire singalong

When Percy is at Camp Half-Blood and not embarking on a quest or recovering from one, this is a typical weekly activity schedule.

CAMP HALF-BLOOD NECKLACES

All the campers are given a leather necklace to wear, with one clay bead on it for every year they have spent at camp. Annabeth's has the most beads because she's been there the longest. When Percy receives his necklace, the bead on it is pitch black with a green trident – marking the year he first entered the camp and the revelation of the identity of his father.

PERCY'S FIRST QUEST

Many campers are envious of Percy because within days of reaching Camp Half-Blood he discovers his identity. Shortly after this, he takes on his first quest and visits the Oracle in the attic of the big house to hear a prophecy.

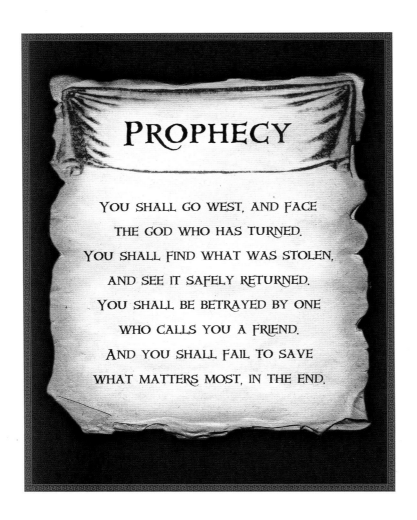

PROPHECY

YOU SHALL GO WEST, AND FACE
THE GOD WHO HAS TURNED.
YOU SHALL FIND WHAT WAS STOLEN,
AND SEE IT SAFELY RETURNED.
YOU SHALL BE BETRAYED BY ONE
WHO CALLS YOU A FRIEND.
AND YOU SHALL FAIL TO SAVE
WHAT MATTERS MOST, IN THE END.

Who's your parent?

If you think you might be a half-blood, try this quiz to see which god might be your parent.

PART ONE

1. What would you rather do for fun?

a) jump out of an airplane
b) go scuba diving
c) work in the garden
d) gossip about who likes who at school

2) What's your favorite color?

a) blood red
b) the color of money!
c) purple
d) black, black and black

3) What would you rather have for your birthday?

a) an electric guitar
b) a tool set
c) a library full of books
d) a hunting trip with friends

PART ONE **RESULTS**

Make a note of the names of the three gods you are linked to by your answers.

*1a Zeus, 1b Poseidon,
1c Demeter, 1d Aphrodite
2a Ares, 2b Hermes,
2c Dionysus, 2d Hades
3a Apollo, 3b Hephaestus,
3c Athena, 3d Artemis*

PART TWO
THE DECIDER

Read the following statements and decide which best describes you. Rate them from 1 to 12, with 1 being the most like you and 12 the least like you. Whichever god scores highest of the three you were linked to in part one is your parent.

1) The undersea world fascinates me and holds the key to life on this planet. Don't try to cross me, or you'll regret it.

2) I believe that reading is one of life's great pleasures, as well as debating with the finest minds of the moment. Weaving is the perfect way to unwind after a hard day's work.

3) I don't take anything from anyone. You want to try something, punk? You'll be sorry.

4) I am incredibly creative. I love music and writing and my fondest wish is to shine!

5) I like to be in charge and tell people what to do. I always enjoy the company of a pretty woman.

6) I want to get ahead in the world. I plan to make a huge amount of money in the business world, and I love to travel.

7) There's nothing compared to the thrill of the chase, followed by an evening under the stars.

8) I am very practical and inventive. With my toolbox I can fix anything and make it good as new.

9) I turn heads wherever I go and spend whole weekends exchanging make-up tips with my girlfriends.

10) Once a party animal, always a party animal - that's me. And I've never been known to walk past a gaming arcade.

11) I'm a homebody, but when I do go out, I like to work invisibly and under the cover of darkness.

12) I have a green thumb and can grow plants anywhere. There's nothing as pleasurable as the feel of good earth in your hands, or as satisfying as providing food for the table.

PART TWO **KEY**

12 Demeter	6 Hermes
11 Hades	5 Zeus
10 Dionysus	4 Apollo
9 Aphrodite	3 Ares
8 Hephaestus	2 Athena
7 Artemis	1 Poseidon

SECTION THREE

GODS
& SPIRITS

THE ULTIMATE GUIDE

THE STORY OF KRONOS

KRONOS WAS KING OF THE TITANS. HE FEARED HE WOULD BE OVERCOME BY THE CHILDREN HE HAD HAD WITH RHEA. SO HE ATE THE CHILDREN. BUT HIS WIFE HID HER LAST BABY, ZEUS, AND GAVE KRONOS A ROCK TO EAT INSTEAD. LATER, WHEN ZEUS GREW UP, HE TRICKED KRONOS BY MAKING HIM EAT A MIXTURE OF MUSTARD AND WINE, SO HE REGURGITATED HIS BROTHERS AND SISTERS. BECAUSE THEY WERE IMMORTAL GODS, THE CHILDREN HAD BEEN LIVING AND GROWING UP UNDIGESTED IN KRONOS'S STOMACH. THERE WAS A BIG FIGHT, WHICH THE GODS WON.

THEY THEN SLICED KRONOS TO PIECES WITH HIS OWN SCYTHE AND SCATTERED WHAT WAS LEFT OF HIM IN TARTARUS, THE DARKEST PART OF THE UNDERWORLD.

ZEUS AND HIS BROTHERS

WITH KRONOS DESTROYED, HIS THREE POWERFUL SONS, ZEUS, POSEIDON, AND HADES, DREW LOTS TO DECIDE WHO WOULD RULE. ZEUS BECAME RULER OF THE SKIES AND KING OF THE GODS IN MOUNT OLYMPUS; POSEIDON RULED THE SEAS; AND HADES RULED THE UNDERWORLD.

THE CYCLOPES (SEE PAGES 52 AND 53) HAD HELPED THE THREE BROTHERS TO DEFEAT KRONOS AND BANISH HIM. THEY GAVE ZEUS THUNDER AND LIGHTNING WITH WHICH HE RULED THE SKIES. TO POSEIDON THEY GAVE A TRIDENT WITH WHICH HE COULD COMMAND THE WAVES. HADES WAS GIVEN A MAGIC HELM WHICH MADE THE WEARER INVISIBLE.

THE CHILDREN OF THE GODS

ZEUS WAS MARRIED TO HERA, BUT HAD MANY CHILDREN WITH OTHER GODDESSES AND MORTALS. POSEIDON AND HADES ALSO FATHERED MANY CHILDREN WITH VARIOUS DIFFERENT GODDESSES AND MORTALS.

THE CHILDREN OF THESE THREE GODS AND MORTAL WOMEN ARE CALLED HALF-BLOODS, OR DEMIGODS. THEY ARE MORE POWERFUL THAN OTHER HALF-BLOODS, AND CAUSE MANY PROBLEMS IN THE WORLD.

AFTER WORLD WAR II, THE THREE BROTHERS TOOK A SOLEMN OATH ON THE RIVER STYX THAT THEY WOULD HAVE NO MORE AFFAIRS WITH MORTAL WOMEN, SO NO MORE POWERFUL DEMIGODS WOULD BE BORN. BUT DID THEY ALL KEEP THIS PROMISE?

THE OLYMPIAN GODS

ZEUS

Zeus was the god of the sky, the supreme god of the Olympians, and ruler of mankind. He was the last child of the Titans Kronos and Rhea, and had five older brothers and sisters (see page 62). Zeus married his sister Hera, but had many love affairs with goddesses and mortals. He punished anyone who lied, though he tried to be fair and keep a balanced view of events. He was responsible for the weather, and when in high spirits, blessed the world with fine weather; in a bad mood he created rain, wind, lightning, and thunder. But even Zeus could not influence the decisions of the Fates. Zeus's symbols are the scales and a thunderbolt. His sacred animal is the eagle.

POSEIDON

Poseidon was the god of the sea. He was the son of the Titans Kronos and Rhea, and brother of Zeus and Hades. His weapon was a trident powerful enough to shake the earth, causing storms and earthquakes. Poseidon had a throne in Mount Olympus and an undersea palace where he usually lived with his wife Amphitrite. His symbol is the trident, and his sacred animals are the dolphin and the horse.

ARES

Ares was the god of war. He was the son of Zeus and Hera, and half-brother to Athena. Ares was a difficult character and unpopular with the other gods and humans. He often fought with Artemis, goddess of the hunt, and with his sister Athena. Ares's symbols are the spear and dogs. Ares had no wife and was constantly under the spell of the goddess Aphrodite, much to the annoyance of her husband Hephaestus. Ares and Aphrodite had four children together. Ares also had many children by mortal women.

"The guy on the bike would've made pro wrestlers run for Mama. He was dressed in a red muscle shirt and black jeans and a black leather duster, with a hunting knife strapped to his thigh. He wore red wraparound shades and he had the cruellest, most brutal face I'd ever seen – handsome, I guess, but wicked – with an oily black crew cut and cheeks that were scarred from many, many fights."

ATHENA

Athena was the goddess of wisdom, skill, and war. She was a child of Zeus and Metis, Zeus's first wife, and was born fully grown, springing out of Zeus's head, wearing full battle armor. She taught humans skills such as weaving, sewing, farming, and metalwork. Her symbols are the olive branch and the owl.

HESTIA

Hestia was the goddess of the hearth, home, and family. She was the eldest daughter of the Titans Kronos and Rhea. Both Poseidon and Apollo wanted to marry her, but she swore to Zeus that she would never marry. Hestia kept the fire burning in every hearth, providing warmth and security. Her symbol is a living flame and her sacred animals are a donkey and pigs.

APHRODITE ▲

Aphrodite was the goddess of love and beauty. She was married to the lame smith Hephaestus but she loved Ares, the god of war. Aphrodite was the most attractive goddess on Mount Olympus. Her symbols are the seashell and the mirror. Her sacred animal is the dove.

APOLLO ▼

Apollo was the god of the sun, prophecy, music and healing. He was the son of Zeus and the mortal Leto, and the younger twin of Artemis, the goddess of the hunt. Famous for playing the lyre, Apollo also had the gift of prophecy. His symbols are the lyre and laurel tree.

ARTEMIS

Artemis was the goddess of the hunt and the moon. She was the daughter of Zeus and Leto and older twin of Apollo, god of the sun. Artemis brought fertility and loved to hunt with a bow and arrows. Her symbol is the bow and her sacred animals are the snake and the deer.

DEMETER

Demeter was the goddess of agriculture, a daughter of the Titans Rhea and Kronos. Her daughter Persephone was taken by Hades to live in the Underworld. Demeter was the source of all growth and life on earth, who taught humans how to cultivate and grow crops. Her symbol is an ear of wheat.

DIONYSUS ▲

Dionysus, the god of wine, was the son of Zeus and the princess Semele. He was known for his lightheartness and always offered to help anyone in need. He did not live in Mount Olympus but constantly traveled the world to discover the secrets of winemaking. His symbols are grapes and ivy and his sacred animal is the panther.

HADES

Hades, ruler of the Underworld and god of the dead, lived with Persephone in the Underworld. The symbol of Hades is a helmet which helped him to stay invisible.

HEPHAESTUS ▶

Hephaestus was god of fire and crafts and of blacksmiths. He was the son of Zeus and Hera and was married to Aphrodite, the goddess of beauty. He was kind and lovable, but also ugly and lame. He had a fiery workshop beneath a volcano in Italy where he worked with the Cyclopes to create thunderbolts for Zeus. The symbols of Hephaestus are fire, the axe, the tongs, and the hammer.

HERA ▼

Hera was the goddess of marriage and the family. She was Zeus's sister and also became his wife. The couple had four children: Eilithyia, the goddess of childbirth; Ares, the god of war; Hebe, the goddess of youth; and Hephaestus, the god of fire and crafts. Hera's sacred animal is the peacock.

HERMES

Hermes was the god of travelers, merchants and thieves, and the messenger of the gods. He was the son of Zeus and the mountain nymph Maea. Hermes had wings on his sandals, which made him the speediest of all the gods. He was the only Olympian god allowed to visit heaven, earth and the Underworld. His symbol is a winged stick with snakes wrapped around it called a caduceus.

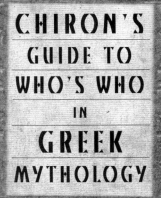

CHIRON'S
GUIDE TO
WHO'S WHO
IN
GREEK
MYTHOLOGY

ZEUS
God of the Sky

DISTINGUISHING FEATURES

Pin-striped suit, neatly-trimmed gray beard, stormy eyes, and a very large, dangerous lightning bolt.

NOW

On stormy days, he can be found brooding in his throne room in Mount Olympus, over the Empire State Building in New York. Sometimes he travels the world in disguise, so be nice to everyone! You never know when the next person you meet might be packing the master bolt.

THEN

In the old days, Zeus ruled over his unruly family of Olympians while they bickered and fought and got jealous of each other. Not much different than today, really. Zeus always had an eye for beautiful women, which often got him in trouble with his wife, Hera. A less-than-stellar father figure, Zeus once tossed Hera's son Hephaestus off the top of Mount Olympus because the baby was too ugly.

POSEIDON
God of the Sea

DISTINGUISHING FEATURES

Colorful Hawaiian shirt, shorts, flip flops, and a three-pointed trident.

NOW

Poseidon walks the beaches of Florida, occasionally stopping to chat with fishermen or take pictures for tourists. If he's in a bad mood, he stirs up a hurricane.

THEN

Poseidon was always a moody guy. On his good days, he did cool stuff like create horses out of sea foam. On his bad days, he caused minor problems like destroying cities with earthquakes, or sinking entire fleets of ships. But hey, a god has the right to throw a temper tantrum, doesn't he?

ARES
God of War

DISTINGUISHING FEATURES

Biker leathers, Harley Davidson, sunglasses, and a stinking attitude.

NOW

Can be found riding his Harley around the suburbs of LA. One of those gods who could pick a fight in an empty room.

THEN

Back in the day, this son of Zeus and Hera used to be inseparable from his shield and helmet. Fought on the side of the Trojans during the war of Troy, but frankly has been involved in every minor skirmish since Goldilocks told the three bears that their beds were a little uncomfy.

ATHENA
Goddess of Wisdom, Skill, and War

DISTINGUISHING FEATURES

Dark hair, striking gray eyes, casual yet fashionable clothes (except when she's going into battle; then it's full body armor). Athena is always accompanied by at least one owl, her sacred (and fortunately housebroken) animal.

NOW

You're likely to spot Athena at an American university, sitting in on lectures about military history or technology. She favors people who invent useful things, and will sometimes appear to reward them with magical gifts or bits of useful advice (like next week's lottery numbers).

THEN

Athena was one of the most active goddesses in human affairs. She helped out Odysseus, sponsored the entire city of Athens, and made sure the Greeks won the Trojan War. On the downside, she's proud and has a big temper. Just ask Arachne, who got turned into a spider for daring to compare her weaving skills to Athena's.

DIONYSUS
God of Wine

DISTINGUISHING FEATURES

Leopard-skin shirt, walking shorts, purple socks and sandals, the general pasty demeanor of someone who has been up partying much too late.

NOW

Dionysus has been sentenced to one hundred years of rehab as director of Camp Half-Blood. The only thing the god of wine can drink these days is Diet Coke, which doesn't make him happy. He can usually be found playing pinochle with a group of terrified satyrs on the front porch of the Big House.

THEN

Dionysus invented wine, which so impressed his father Zeus that he made Dionysus a god. He mostly spent his time partying it up in ancient Greece, but once a crew of sailors tried to kill him, thinking the god was too incapacitated to fight back. Dionysus turned them into dolphins and sent them over the side. The moral of this story: do not mess with a god, even a drunk one.

HERMES
God of Travelers, Merchants, and Thieves

DISTINGUISHING FEATURES

Jogger's clothes and winged athletic shoes, a cell phone that turns into the caduceus, his symbol of power — a winged staff with two snakes, entwined around it.

NOW

Hermes is a hard person to find, because he's always on the run. When he's not delivering messages for the gods, he's running a telecommunications company, an express delivery service, and every other type of business you can imagine that involves travel. Did you have a question about his activities as god of thieves? Leave a message. He'll get back to you in a few millennia.

THEN

Hermes got started young as a troublemaker. When he was one day old, he stole some cattle from his brother Apollo. Apollo probably would've blasted the tyke to bits, but fortunately Hermes appeased him with a new musical instrument he'd created called the lyre, which made Apollo very popular with the ladies.

MINOR GODS AND SPIRITS

THE CHARITES

The Charites were three goddesses of grace, beauty, joy, festivity, dance and song. They usually attended Aphrodite, the goddess of beauty, and Hera, the goddess of marriage. The Charites loved dancing in a circle to Apollo's divine music, together with the Nymphs and the Muses.

THE MUSES

The Muses were the goddesses of music, song, and dance, and the source of inspiration to poets. They were also goddesses of knowledge, who remembered everything that had happened. The Muses often accompanied the Charites in their singing and dancing.

THE NYMPHS

The Nymphs were female spirits of the natural world, minor goddesses of the forests, rivers, springs, meadows, mountains and seas. They were responsible for the beauty of nature. The Nymphs were the daughters of Zeus. They wandered through groves

◀ NYMPHS

of trees and lived near springs, in mountains through which rivers flowed, and in woods. The Nymphs played with the gods Artemis and Apollo and especially Hermes and the satyr Pan.

THE WINDS

The Winds, or Anemoi, were the gods of the four directional winds: Boreas the north wind, Zephryos the west wind, Notos the south wind, and Euros the east wind. They were connected with the seasons:

Boreas was the cold breath of winter, Zephyros the god of spring breezes, and Notos the god of summer rainstorms. The Winds were winged gods with a human form and were created by Astraeus, the god of the stars, and Eos, the goddess of the dawn.

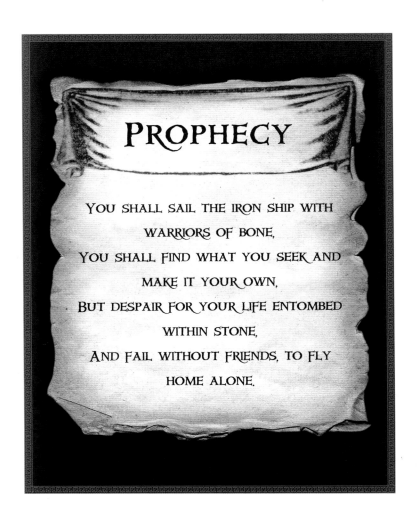

PROPHECY

YOU SHALL SAIL THE IRON SHIP WITH

WARRIORS OF BONE,

YOU SHALL FIND WHAT YOU SEEK AND

MAKE IT YOUR OWN,

BUT DESPAIR FOR YOUR LIFE ENTOMBED

WITHIN STONE,

AND FAIL WITHOUT FRIENDS, TO FLY

HOME ALONE.

GODS OF THE SEA

NEREUS

Nereus was the old man of the sea and the god of the sea's rich bounty of fish. He lived at the bottom of the Aegean in a magnificent palace built inside a cave. Nereus was a master shapeshifter and always spoke the truth. He had the tail of a fish, the torso of a man, a beard, and hair as white as sea foam. Nereus married Doris, a daughter of Oceanus, the Titan of the seas. They had fifty beautiful mermaids called the Nereids, who protected sailors with their sweet, enchanting voices.

PROTEUS

Proteus was the son of Poseidon and the herdsman of his seals.

He knew every sea and could change into any animal. Although he had the gift of prophecy, he would not reveal the truth about the future unless he was captured.

TRITON

The sea god Triton, son of Poseidon and Amphitrite, served as Poseidon's messenger. He had the shape of a merman: the head and torso of a man and the tail of a fish. He carried a horn or conch shell which he blew.

Triton had enormous power and could move whole islands or calm seas. He took part in the battle of the Olympian gods against the giants, helping to chase them away. Like Proteus and Nereus, Triton possessed the gift of prophecy.

MINOR GODS

ADONIS

Adonis was a handsome young hunter who was loved by the goddess Aphrodite. When he was a baby, Aphrodite put him in a chest and entrusted his care to Persephone, goddess of the Underworld. Persephone fell under the spell of Adonis's beauty and refused to return him when he became a man. Eventually it was decided that Persephone should keep Adonis in the Underworld for four months every year. He would also spend four months with Aphrodite and stay with whomever he chose for the remaining four months. However, he chose to stay with Aphrodite.

NEMESIS

Nemesis was the goddess of retribution and a symbol of justice. She had to measure out and maintain a balance between happiness and unhappiness, making sure that neither was too frequent or too great.

PERSEPHONE

Persephone, goddess of the Underworld, was the

daughter of Zeus and Demeter, the goddess of agriculture.

One day Hades fell in love with her and carried her away to the Underworld. When Demeter learned what had happened, she was so furious that she left Mount Olympus and stopped everything on earth from growing.

Zeus decided to bring Persephone back to her mother and sent Hermes to fetch her. But before Hades released Persephone, he gave her seven seeds of pomegranate to eat, so that she was forever connected to the Underworld and would stay there for four months every year.

This is how the seasons were created: when Persephone was with Demeter, the sun shone and everything flowered. The rest of the time Demeter grieved and winter gripped the world.

STYX

Styx was the eldest of the three thousand daughters of the Titans Oceanus and Tethys. She and her children played an important role in the battle against the Titans, and so she was honored by Zeus and became the goddess of the River Styx. The river separated the world of the living from the world of the dead; the Olympian gods swore by its waters when making oaths.

NYX

Nyx was the goddess of the night. She lived in Tartarus, in the depths of the Underworld and shared her house with her daughter Hemera, who was her opposite and symbolized the day.

▲ RIVER STYX

SECTION FOUR

PERCY JACKSON'S BESTIARY

THE ULTIMATE GUIDE

▲ CERBERUS

BEASTS AND MONSTERS

AETHIOPIAN DRAKON

A giant African serpent with rows of sharp teeth.

AGRIUS & OREIUS (BEAR-MEN)

Twin sons of a human and a bear. Eight feet tall, with furry chests, claws for fingernails, and paws for feet, snout-like noses and sharp canine teeth. Luke Castellan's henchmen.

CARNIVOROUS SHEEP

Sheep the size of hippos on Polyphemus's island, which eat other animals.

CENTAURS

Creatures with the head and torso of a man and the body of a horse, see page 39. Called on by Chiron at times of crisis, they gallop to the rescue armed with paintball guns.

CERBERUS

Huge black Rottweiler, twice the size of a wooly mammoth, with three heads. The hound of Hades who guards the entrance to the Underworld and prevents the dead from leaving.

CHARYBDIS

One of the monsters who guards the entrance to the Sea of Monsters. To stop sailors entering, she sucks up the sea and everything in it.

CHERRY-COLOR COWS

Red cattle sacred to Apollo on the Triple G Ranch.

CHIMERA ▼

Huge monster with the head of a lion, a blood-caked mane, the body and hooves of giant goat. Its tail is a ten-foot-long diamondback snake which grows out of its shaggy behind. Breathes fire.

CHIMERA

CLAZMONIAN SOW

Enormous winged female pig with flamingo-pink wings that destroys all in its path and belches poison gas.

CRAB ▶

Ten-foot-tall monster crab with mottled blue and green shell and nasty pincers longer than a man's body.

ECHIDNA

Monstrous snake woman with a human head and snake-like body. Has a forked tongue, vicious fangs, green scaly skin and the eyes of a reptile.

EMPOUSAE

Horrifying creatures of the Underworld that feed on human flesh. Often appear in mortal form as mean cheerleaders

ERYMANTHIAN BOAR

Thirty-foot-high wild boar with tusks the size of canoes. Can move extremely fast, so better used as a form of transport than confronted head on.

FLESH-EATING HORSES

Frightening horses that eat the flesh of other creatures and live in great piles of horse poop. Ideal for garbage disposal, but a challenge to clean out.

FURIES

See page 20.

GUINEA PIGS

Enchanted sailors on Circe's magic island in the Sea of Monsters.

HEKATONKHEIRES

(Hundred-handed ones) Giant gods of violent storms and hurricanes and elder brothers of the Cyclopes. Each had a hundred hands and fifty heads. Ideal to have on your side when assaulting enemies with rocks.

HELLHOUNDS

Huge dogs from hell, with black fur, glowing red eyes, massive strength and speed, and the ability to appear and disappear at will. Almost all are unfriendly to demigods, with the exception of Mrs. O'Leary, pet to Quintus. She is bigger than a tank, has a bark slightly louder than an artillery gun and can shadow travel.

HIPPALEKTRYONS

Creatures with the front half of a horse and the back half of a rooster. Their rear feet have huge yellow claws and they have feathery tails and red wings.

HIPPOCAMPI

Sea creatures with the front half of a horse and the back half of a silvery fish, with glistening scales and rainbow tail fins.

HYDRA

A scaly monster with nine heads, each one diamond-shaped with a mouth lined with jagged teeth. Each

mouth spits poison. If one of its heads is severed, the hydra grows two heads in place of the lost one.

HYPERBOREAN GIANTS

Thirty-foot tall giants with blue skin and ice-gray hair.

◄ KAMPÊ

A creature with the top half of a woman and the body of a dragon. The dragon body is twenty feet long, black and scaly, with enormous claws and a barbed tail. Kampê's legs and hair sprout vipers.

LADON

Enormous, many-headed dragon that guards the golden apples of the Hesperides sisters. Has hundreds of heads.

LAISTRYGONIAN GIANTS ►

Eight-foot-tall cannibal giants with tattooed arms,

yellow pointed teeth, leather armor. Carry heavy, spiked clubs.

LYDIAN DRAKON

Poisonous giant serpent with scales harder than titanium and eyes that paralyze.

◀ MANTICORE

Has the body of a lion, a human face and a leathery, spiky tail which shoots out deadly thorns, like crossbow bolts.

MINOTAUR

Half-man, half bull monster. See page 27, illustrated page 107.

NEMEAN LION

A lion as big as a pick-up truck with silver claws and golden, glittering fur.

OPHIOTAURUS

"Bessie," a sea creature with the front half of a calf and the back half of a serpent. The fate of the gods and Mount Olympus rests on him.

ORTHUS

A dog with sleek brown hair and two heads. Guard dog at the Triple G Ranch.

PEGASI (see page 39)

Powerful winged horses created by Poseidon.

Blackjack, Percy's steed, is a gleaming black stallion who helps the demigods in their quests.

PELEUS

Guardian dragon of Camp Half-Blood. Huge and coppery-scaled, he sleeps coiled around the pine tree at the top of the hill.

PIT SCORPIONS ▼

Deadly insects about the size of a hand. Can jump up to fifteen feet, and their stingers pierce through clothes. Their poison can kill within sixty seconds.

▲ MINOTAUR

down and pluck sailors from their ships.

◄ SCYTHIAN DRACAENAE

Dragon women with green scaly skin, yellow eyes and two tails instead of legs.

SIRENS

People-sized vultures with black plumage, wrinkled pink necks and human faces.

SCYLLA

Monster who guards the entrance to the Sea of Monsters. Has six heads on long necks which reach

SPHINX

Monster with the body of a huge lion and the head of a woman. Huge paws have claws like stainless steel.

STYMPHALIAN BIRDS

Man-eating demon birds with evil, beady eyes and razor-sharp bronze beaks. Reputed to strip anything they attack to bones. Can only be defeated by horrible sounds.

TELEKHINES

Six-foot tall sea demons who are metal-workers and make many of the gods' weapons. Have the faces of dogs, with black snouts, brown eyes and pointed ears. Their bodies are sleek and black with stubby legs which are half flipper, half foot. Their humanlike hands have sharp claws.

Resemble a cross between a kid, a Doberman pinscher and a sea lion.

TYPHON

An enormous monster once trapped by the gods under a mountain. Human-shaped with mottled green skin, human hands, the talons of an eagle and scaly, reptilian legs. Once released, Typhon caused swathes of devastation.

WOLVES

White timber wolves that accompany the hunters of Artemis.

ENTER

CAN YOU ESCAPE THE LABYRINTH?

SOLUTION: PAGE 119

ESCAPE!

SECTION FIVE

THE LABYRINTH

THE ULTIMATE GUIDE

ENCOUNTERS IN THE LABYRINTH

On their quest in the labyrinth, Percy, Annabeth, Tyson, and Grover search for Daedalus's workshop.

THE TWO-FACED MAN

They meet a man with two faces, standing in front of two doors. Both faces speak to Annabeth, and demand that she choose the right door to open with a silver key. But which is the right door? The strange doorkeeper is Janus, the god of doorways, beginnings, endings and choices, who looks to both the future and the past. Annabeth is rescued from her dilemma by the goddess Hera, who offers them advice on how to find Daedalus in the Labyrinth.

ENDING UP IN JAIL

The questers find themselves in a tunnel which ends inside Alcatraz Prison in California, where they encounter the imprisoned Briares (a "hundred-handed one").

A History of Alcatraz

The US army built a military fortress on Alcatraz Island in 1853, and in 1861, installed long-range cannons that could sink hostile ships three miles away. In 1861 the island also began taking prisoners from the Civil War, and by 1898 it had more than 450 inmates. In 1906 hundreds of civilian prisoners were transferred to the island after the San Franscisco earthquake, and by 1912 a large cellhouse had been constructed. Alcatraz had a reputation for being a tough prison that treated inmates to harsh confinement and iron discipline. The prison closed in 1934, but it was modernized and reopened by the Department of Justice later that year to hold the gangsters and criminals who were part of the crime surge sparked by the Great Depression. The prison was nicknamed "Devil's Island". Famous inmates included Al Capone, Robert Stroud (the "Birdman of Alcatraz") and George "Machine Gun" Kelly. Alcatraz prison was closed in 1963.

Once powerful, Briares has been overwhelmed by years of imprisonment and fears the revenge of the monster Kampê should he attempt to escape.

TRIPLE G RANCH

The four questers find a grate that brings them to a ranch where they encounter Orthus, the two-headed dog (see page 110) and Eurytion the cowherd, who suggests they turn right around and go back into the Labyrinth while they have the chance. When they refuse, he takes them to meet the boss, Geryon, who turns out to have no less than three bodies:

"His neck connected to the middle chest... but he had two more chests, one to either side, connected at the shoulders, with a few inches in between. His left arm grew out of his left chest, and the same on the right, so he had two arms, but four armpits... The chests all connected into one enormous torso, with two regular but very beefy legs, and he wore the most oversized pair of Levis I'd ever seen."

The extraordinary animals raised on Triple G Ranch include hippalektryons and hideous flesh-eating horses (see Bestiary).

◀ GERYON

DAEDALUS'S WORKSHOP

LABYRINTH SOLUTION

SECTION SIX

THE
UNDERWORLD

THE ULTIMATE GUIDE

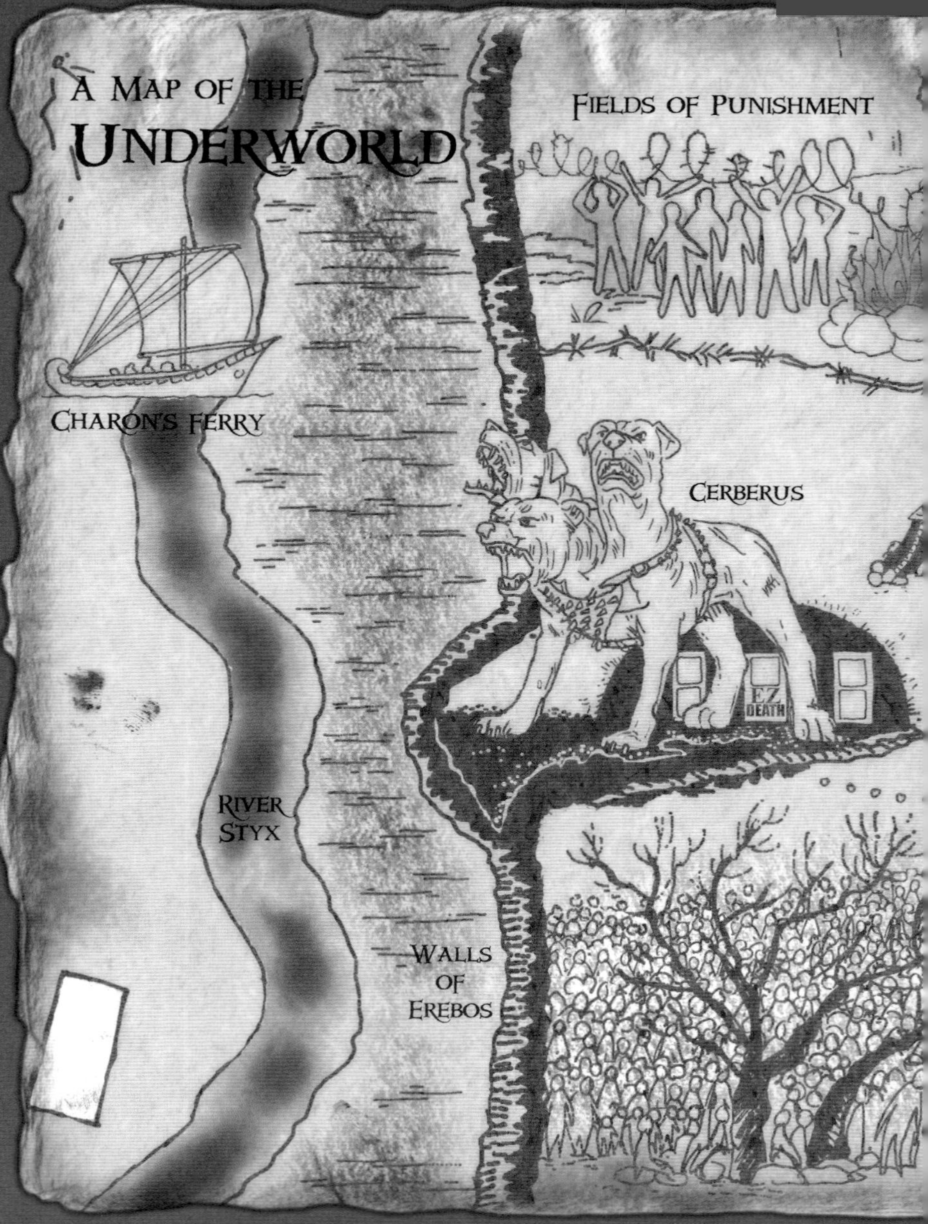

A MAP OF THE
UNDERWORLD

FIELDS OF PUNISHMENT

CHARON'S FERRY

CERBERUS

RIVER
STYX

EZ
DEATH

WALLS
OF
EREBOS

A GUIDED TOUR OF THE UNDERWORLD *by Nico di Angelo*

"Hi! Welcome to my dad's place. My name's Nico di Angelo, son of Hades. Let me show you around....

"You met Cerberus when you came in, right? Good guard dog, yeah? No one gets past those three heads without an official escort. This path takes you straight to the Judgment Pavilion. Ignore all these silent types we're wading through – they're dead – they can't bother you. Note the wicked black grass and trees we have here in the Fields of Asphodel – and don't miss the stunning stalactites – that's what they'll do to you if one of them breaks off the ceiling and spears you!

"OK – this is the pavilion where all the newly-dead have to go: as it says on the banner, they're here for JUDGMENTS FOR ELYSIUM AND ETERNAL DAMNATION. Poor chumps! Cool black tent though, right?

"Come right on through and see what happens after they've been processed. That path to the left goes straight to the Fields of Punishment – the name says it all. That's where

Dad tries out his new punishment ideas, but he says the traditional ones still work best: the lava flows, the minefields full of exploding surprises, burning at the stake, running naked through cactus patches... You name it, we've got it here.

"Anyone not feeling well should sit down on this bench here and put their heads between their legs until the nausea passes.

"Now let's take a look at where the right-hand path leads – this one should be easier for you live folks to stomach. Through those security gates is Elysium, where I guess you all want to end up one day. We have neighborhoods from way back in history – you name it, we've got it: Roman, medieval, Victorian. Check the gold and silver flowers – better than up there, I bet. Year-round barbecues too – can't be bad.

"See that gleaming blue lake in the middle there, with the three little islands? Those are the Isles of the Blest – folks that end up on those islands have chosen to be reborn three times and each time have achieved Elysium. Bet you wouldn't mind joining them. Keep on the straight and narrow, that's what they say. You can see how hard it is to do that – look at the tiny size of Elysium compared to the Fields of Asphodel and Punishment.

"Now drag yourselves away and I'll take you to Dad's palace. You haven't seen anything yet. See those black parapets on the horizon? That's where we're heading. Step on it! Those three batlike creatures hovering around you are the Furies – it's better not to get on their bad side.

"No one take that path down to the right. Unless you want an unscheduled visit to Tartarus, that is.

"Here we are at the palace. The walls are polished obsidian – you can practically see yourself reflected in them. Notice the height of these automatic bronze gates and the intricate carvings on them. Dad's got images of pretty much all the different ways a human can die. This one here's an atom bomb exploding, there's a row of famine victims, trenches from World War I – there's nothing he's missed as far as I can see.

"Now this is a special Underworld garden! Nothing growing here needs natural light – that's why we have mushrooms and luminous plants which don't need

TARTARUS

TARTARUS IS THE DEEPEST REGION OF THE WORLD, UNDER THE UNDERWORLD ITSELF. IT IS SO FAR DOWN THAT AN ANVIL THROWN FROM HEAVEN WOULD TAKE NINE DAYS TO REACH IT. THE SOULS OF THE MOST WICKED WERE SENTENCED TO ETERNAL TORMENT HERE. IT IS AN ABYSS SURROUNDED BY WALLS AND GATES OF BRONZE FROM WHICH NO ONE MAY ESCAPE.

TANTALUS

ZEUS'S SON TANTALUS WAS IMPRISONED IN TARTARUS FOR TRYING TO SERVE THE GODS A DISH OF HUMAN FLESH. HIS PUNISHMENT WAS TO BE KEPT PERMANENTLY HUNGRY AND THIRSTY WHILE STANDING CHIN-DEEP IN WATER WITH FRUIT HANGING FROM BRANCHES JUST ABOVE HIS HEAD. WHENEVER HE TRIED TO DRINK THE WATER OR EAT THE FRUIT THEY RECEDED JUST BEYOND HIS REACH. THIS IS WHERE THE WORD "TANTALIZE" COMES FROM.

daylight. *And my dad grows precious stones rather than flowers. These are rubies, this pile is diamonds – so much easier than those plants you guys have to water all the time. Now nobody step out of line and everyone do exactly as I say, or you could end up like one of these statues you see around you, gifts from Medusa. As I mentioned before, it's a good idea to stay on the good side of my dad and his friends.*

"This orchard is the garden of Persephone (see pages 90 and 91). *Keep walking and don't touch those pomegranates or you'll never be able to leave.*

Hades allows tour parties only as far as his hallway, so stay together and don't try exploring further, unless you'd enjoy being locked up here for the rest of your lives. Meet my dad's guards; nothing gets past them. They may look like skeletons, but they can kill as well as anyone alive upstairs.

"OK, well that just about wraps up the tour for today. Follow me back to the entrance and gift shop where you can buy souvenirs of your visit. And don't forget, the tour is free, but you need five golden drachmas to buy your exit permit. This way to the return tour ferry…"

THE STOREHOUSE OF THE GODS

ARTIFACTS AND CURIOSITIES

AEGIS

The silver chain bracelet worn by Thalia. When tapped it expands into a huge shield. A gift from Athena, the shield is made from silver and bronze, with the monstrous face of Medusa protruding from the middle. It gives off a powerful petrifying aura.

AMBROSIA

The healing god food used in emergencies when demigods are seriously hurt. Ambrosia will cure almost any injury, although too much can make a demigod feverish and kills mortals. At Camp Half-Blood ambrosia comes in squares in sealed bags. On Mount Olympus you can buy it on a stick.

ANAKLUSMOS

Percy's sword, which translates as Riptide. The sword turns from an ordinary disposable ballpoint (with black ink) into a shimmering, double-edged bronze sword. It has a leather-wrapped grip and a flat hilt riveted with gold studs and always returns to Percy's pocket moments after it has left his grasp.

BASKETBALL SHOES

Shoes given by Luke to Percy for his first quest. On the call "Maia," white bird's wings sprout from the heels.

BACKBITER ▼

Luke's sword which has one celestial bronze and one tempered steel edge so it works on both mortals and immortals. Was first used by Kronos to slice up his father Ouranos.

CELESTIAL BRONZE KNIFE

The knife that Luke gave to Annabeth when they first met as children on the street.

CHARIOTS

Chariot races were reintroduced at Camp Half-Blood by Tantalus.

GOLDEN DRACHMAS

Ancient Greek currency used by demigods to pay for rainbow messages to contact their friends and relatives.

DINOSAUR TEETH

Used by the General to grow fearsome skeleton warriors who relentlessly pursue their targets.

GOLDEN FLEECE

The golden ram skin which brings health to all it touches.

GREEK FIRE

A thick green magical liquid which billows green smoke and then explodes. Used by demigods when fighting monsters.

HADES'S HELM OF DARKNESS

A ski cap that transforms into an elaborate bronze war helmet. The helmet was made for Hades by the Cyclopes.

INVISIBILITY CAP

A navy Yankees baseball cap, given to Annabeth by Athena for her twelfth birthday. It renders the wearer invisible.

PANDORA'S PITHOS

A storage jar, also called Pandora's box, which held evil, illness and hardship. Although told not to open it, Pandora was overcome by curiosity and did.

JAVELINS

Made by Tyson for Percy and Annabeth to use in a Camp chariot race.

NECTAR

The drink of the gods, used alongside Ambrosia for healing. Always tastes of the drinker's favorite food. At the gods' parties on Mount Olympus, both nectar and ambrosia come out of golden fountains.

REED PIPES

The pan pipes played by satyrs. Used for various purposes including tracking and banishing pests. See pages 49 and 50.

VIDEO SHIELD

Reflects surroundings. Made for Annabeth based on an idea of Daedalus's.

STYGIAN DOG WHISTLE

A special dog whistle given to Percy by Quintus so he

could summon the friendly hellhound Mrs. O'Leary in an emergency. The whistle was made of ice from the River Styx, and very cold. It shattered into shards of ice when blown.

MIST

Conjured by gods and demigods in order to pull the wool over mortal eyes. This prevents humans from either seeing or remembering events.

WRISTWATCH SHIELD

A shield made for Percy which expands from a wristwatch when he pushes the stopwatch button.

YELLOW DUFFEL BAGS

Three magical waterproof bags Hermes gave to Percy, Annabeth and Tyson for their sea journey.

AUTOMATA

COLCHIS BULLS
Fiery metal bulls with fist-sized rubies for eyes and horns of polished silver. Breathe white-hot flame from their hinged metal mouths. Made by Hephaestus.

SKELETON WARRIORS
Skeletal warriors conjured by Atlas to attack Percy and the other demigods.

GUARDIANS

Two winged bronze statues at the Hoover Dam, who come to the aid of Percy, Thalia, Grover, and Zoë.

METAL SPIDER
A silver disc that turns into a mechanical spider at the press of a button and guides Annabeth and Percy to the underground forges of Hephaestus.

TALOS

A bronze giant the size of a skyscaper in Greek battle armor. Discovered by the demigods in the junkyard of the gods and eventually destroyed by Bianca di Angelo.

MECHANICAL STATUES

Statues in New York that were brought to life by Annabeth after studying Daedalus's ideas for defending Manhattan from attack. They are automatons programmed to activate each other in a chain reaction.

WILLIAM H. SEWARD, MECHANICAL STATUE ▲

SECTION EIGHT

COMPENDIUM

THE ULTIMATE GUIDE

MORTALS WHO SEE THROUGH THE MIST

RACHEL ELIZABETH DARE ▶

Mortal girl whom Percy encountered at the Hoover Dam, and whose quick thinking helped him escape from the skeleton warriors. Green-eyed, with frizzy reddish-brown hair. Wears large, ragged sweatshirts and paint-stained jeans. Rachel loves art and played a key role in one quest, ultimately finding her true role in life in *The Last Olympian*.

DR. CHASE

Annabeth's father.
A professor of military history who collects old planes. Sandy-colored hair and intense brown eyes. Helped Percy and Thalia when they were trying to rescue Annabeth. His old plane came in handy.

MAY CASTELLAN

Luke's mother. After having Luke with Hermes, applied for a job which seriously affected her mental health, and has never been the same since. This was one reason that Luke left home at an early age.

PAUL BLOFIS

Bearded English teacher who fell in love with Percy's mom, Sally Jackson. Salt and pepper hair, denim clothes and leather jacket.

MORE CHARACTERS

PAN

Grover Underwood devoted much of his life to searching for the great god Pan, just as his father and uncle had before him. Pan was a satyr who was the son of Hermes. He was lord of the wild, the god of shepherds and flocks, of wild mountains, hunting

and folk music. Pan disappeared two thousand years ago and a sailor heard a voice calling out that he had died. The satyrs looked up to Pan as their lord and master who protected them and the wild places of the earth and they refuse to believe he really died. So the bravest satyrs in each generation continued the search for him, hoping to wake him from sleep.

◄ HYPERION

The lord of light and Titan of the East – the most powerful of the four Titans who controlled the corners of the world and the father of Helios, the first sun god. A warrior in golden armor with miniature suns for eyes, capable of exuding blinding light.

PROMETHEUS ▼

The Titan god of forethought and crafty counsel, fire-bringer and brother of Atlas.

Prometheus made the first men out of clay and taught them architecture, astronomy, navigation, and medicine. He stole fire from the gods and gave it to the humans. Zeus punished him by chaining him to a rock where an eagle pecked at him. He was eventually freed by the hero Hercules.

ATLAS

A Titan who stood for endurance. He rebelled against Zeus and was condemned to hold up the sky at the point at which it first met the earth. Atlas is Lord Kronos's senior commander.

POLYPHEMUS

A fifteen-foot-tall Cyclops who lived in a cave on an island in the Sea of Monsters. He owned a flock of fearsome carnivorous sheep, who guarded the stolen Golden Fleece which he used to lure satyrs to his island, trap and eat them.

MORPHEUS ▶

The god of dreams and the son of Hypnos, the god of sleep. He sends images to humans in dreams and can shape people's dreams. He can also put whole sections of a city into a dreamlike state.

PROPHECY

Seven half-bloods shall
answer the call.
To storm or fire, the world
must fall.
An oath to keep with a final
breath,
And foes bear arms to the
Doors of Death.